Edinburgh

By

Allan Wright

Contents

Edinburgh

Preface

I have been photographing the city of Edinburgh on and off for about 20 years, and it is with satisfaction that I present a collection of my favourite images, perhaps somewhat loosely collated more as an inspired ramble than a comprehensive account.

I have lingering memories from childhood times spent in the city: the cold sharp air, the wafting aroma of malt and hops, maroon buses, picnics at the Botanic Gardens and the Scott Monument. My appreciation of the grandeur and utterly compelling architecture of Edinburgh came much later.

In 2005 I took some time to examine the city in more penetrating detail. I walked and cycled the streets from sun-up to sundown for days on end with a single-minded hunger. Little treasures were harvested from wherever they might be hiding, sometimes through sheer good fortune, and at other times by stubborn and calculated persistence.

Some of the most enjoyable times for me have been on the streets of Edinburgh during the tourist off-season. The Edinburgh folk seem to repossess their city, and to savour its rich ambience without the sound of bagpipes and noisy gangs of foreign teenagers. I sensed that they were well aware of this pleasure. At these times it became perfectly clear to me why people want to live here. It is so very much more than a tourist destination.

Allan Wright

February 2006

Introduction

The emergence of any city is intriguing. But to discover that the location of the city of Edinburgh has been continuously inhabited for 7,000 years is indeed astonishing – even if archaeological remains are somewhat scant. Over the centuries, achievements in every field of human endeavour have contributed to the emergence of this beautiful city. After the Second World War in 1947, there was a feeling amongst many that the war had not solved any problems: rather, it had increased them. The inspiration to hold an Edinburgh Festival, therefore, proved to be more profitable in every way than any war. The Festival has now been running successfully for nearly sixty years, and has a worldwide reputation.

When a city is as spectacular as Edinburgh, with its old buildings and majestic scenery, there is no better way to expose it than by beautiful photography. Allan Wright's superb photography demonstrates that it is possible to capture the present – with all its modern art and enterprise – without losing the spirit of bygone days. Traditionally, it is said that Edinburgh was built on seven hills. This might account for the many churches and pubs that abound throughout the city – due, no doubt, to the exertion of going up and down the hills giving rise to a need for stimulation!

Geographically Edinburgh is unique in many ways. About 325 million years ago, the renowned 'Edinburgh Volcano' eruption resulted in the emergence of Castle Rock and Arthur's Seat, with lava flows that eventually brought into being Calton Hill and igneous sills like Salisbury Crags and Blackford Hill. After the Ice Age, the Pentland Hills emerged from the ice-floes on the south-western perimeter of the city, followed by deep hollows that eventually formed the Grassmarket, Cowgate and Princes Street Gardens. Atop the splendour of Castle Rock stands Edinburgh Castle: a magnificent presence that holds a silent memory of 'Auld Reekie', as Edinburgh was once known. In spite of its past history, the Castle still dominates most of the city.

It is well worth climbing Arthur's Seat to see the panoramic view over the whole city and observe the extensive formation of the land within and around this landscape. From here, all the landmarks of the city can easily be recognised. It is surprising how different Edinburgh appears from this height. On a clear day, the two famous bridges across the Firth of Forth are visible, together with most of the Fife coast. Within the immediate vicinity of Arthur's Seat are three lochs, one of which is a nature reserve where many birds come to nest in the reeds each year. In the smaller loch in Holyrood Park, swans and geese come to feed on the surrounding grasslands, in spite of the citizens of Edinburgh bringing them titbits.

One great attraction of the Edinburgh Festival is the Edinburgh Military Tattoo. Many different regiments from overseas take part in this parade every year on the Castle Esplanade, together with Scottish and English regiments, regimental bands, pipe bands and a variety of entertainment. The lone piper steals the show with his impressive appearance at the close of every performance. Standing on the Castle balcony, high up above the heads of the crowded arena, he plays the 'Last Lament' – the climax of the Tattoo. The haunting melody moves across the heads of the hushed and vast audience. On the last day of the Festival a magnificent firework display lights up the whole of the city.

Below the Castle are Princes Street Gardens, in what used to be the site of the purpose-built Nor' Loch. On the North side of Princes Street are the shops, hotels and restaurants. An interesting story reveals that, after the Nor' Loch had been reclaimed in about 1805, the Council decided to develop Princes Street still further by selling plots on the south side of the street. The occupants of the north side realised to their horror that any buildings erected on the south side would block their view of the Castle and gardens. They immediately raised an action against the town council – which unfortunately failed in the Scottish Courts. However, when the case came up in the House of Lords, Lord Mansfield, son of the 5th Viscount of Scone, Perthshire, who happened to be at that time the

Lord Chief Justice of England, reversed the judgement, 'incensed by the misguided Corporation and their lack of concern for public interest'.

Soaring 200ft above Princes Street, the greatest thoroughfare in Scotland, is the Scott Monument, built in 1840–6. This fine Neo-Gothic steeple, dedicated to Sir Walter Scott, overlooks Princes Street Gardens, and is perhaps the finest memorial raised to any writer. Close by is the National Gallery of Scotland, behind which is the Royal Scottish Academy. These impressive buildings stand at the foot of The Mound by Princes Street Gardens, where the tallest buildings in Old Edinburgh can be seen towering above Princes Street. Over the centuries, Edinburgh has been the birthplace and home of many famous people who have contributed to the city's distinguished reputation for art and literature. It is partly because of these illustrious inhabitants that Edinburgh has earned the title of 'the Athens of the North'.

The medical profession in Edinburgh has an intriguing history. In 1505, the town council of Edinburgh granted a Charter of Privileges to enable doctors to practise surgery within the city boundaries. In 1694, surgeons were granted sole control of surgery in south-east Scotland. This enforced a need for teaching anatomy. As a result, a purpose-built Surgeon's Hall was opened. It is now part of the University of Edinburgh, and includes the departments of Oral Medicine and Oral Pathology. Many changes followed after the Second World War. The medical school has expanded considerably and it now has Fellows in all parts of the world. From around the 17th to the 19th centuries there were over 1,100 students of the University of Edinburgh studying medicine. It soon became the most important medical school in the world. The increasing number of students meant that there was a growing demand for human bodies for dissection. However, the law had not changed since the charter in 1505, which allowed only one corpse for dissection per year. The escalating need for bodies gave rise to the phenomenon of 'body snatching', in which freshly-buried corpses were dug up and sold to medical students and departments of anatomy by criminals known as 'resurrections'. This gruesome story further reveals that two notorious Ulster criminals, William Burke and William Hare, saw an opportunity for making easy money and developed a method of suffocating live victims so as to leave no trace of violence. They thus succeeded in selling sixteen bodies to the medical students of Edinburgh before they were finally arrested.

Not only is Edinburgh the capital of Scotland, but also it was the second city in Great Britain to procure a Botanic Garden (the first being Oxford). It was originally a Physic Garden established in 1670 by two Scottish doctors. After an interesting history, it developed into a Botanic Garden, and in 1820 eventually moved to its magnificent site in Inverleith Row. In 1888 the Botanic Garden came under the control of the Crown, although it retained its primary importance as a botanical research institution. The layout of the Edinburgh Royal Botanic Garden is superb, with many beautiful trees shading the grasslands and walkways. More recently, a Chinese Pagoda with accompanying waterfall has been added, which blends very well with the scenery and feels rather like a secret garden.

The Grassmarket of the Old Town is still a central meeting place overlooked by the Castle. Markets are still held there to this day, but gone are the gruesome sights of bygone days when criminals could be seen held in stocks or hanged there. The famous Porteous Riots ended in the hanging of Captain John Porteous in the Grassmarket in 1736, when mob rule erupted, overcoming the whims of the rich and powerful. Queen Caroline, in the absence of Henry II, had given Porteous a reprieve, which infuriated the public. Angry crowds stormed the Tolbooth in the High Street where Porteous was imprisoned, and he was dragged, screaming for mercy, to the Grassmarket where he was swiftly hanged. In spite of extensive enquiries, the ringleaders of the riot were never discovered. Leading up from the Grassmarket is the remainder of the Flodden Wall, built in 1513 as a means of protection against English intruders attacking the City.

The Royal Mile is the oldest street in Edinburgh, and is renowned for housing some of the city's finest buildings, closes and wynds. The Royal Mile makes its way down from the Castle to the Palace. The most prominent building is St Giles Cathedral, with its famous Crown Spire dating from the 15th Century. The cathedral lies adjacent to the Old Scottish Parliament. In 1996, a magnificent stained-glass window was placed within the cathedral in memory of Robert Burns (1759–1796), the greatest Scottish Bard. Opposite St Giles is the City Chambers, beneath which is the Real Mary King's Close. You can walk under the City Chambers all the way down alongside Cockburn Street to emerge near Waverley Station, wherein many aspects of Old Edinburgh can be seen, such as relics from the 16th and 17th centuries – plus a few ghosts! The Royal Mile eventually ends at the Palace of Holyroodhouse. In 1534, the Palace and the adjacent Abbey were nearly reduced to ashes by the English. The Palace and Church were rebuilt, but later fell again into near-ruins by fire. Eventually the Stuart Kings, James V and VI, restored the Palace once more. The Abbey Church, however, remains in ruins.

When James VI of Scotland became James I of England, the Union of the Crowns made it impossible for the Old Scottish Parliament to survive, particularly as a number of influential supporters of the monarchy made a surreptitious agreement that decided the Union of the Scottish and English Parliaments. However, the Scottish Law Lords demanded that Scotland should retain their jurisdiction in Edinburgh over the Scottish Courts of Justice and be allowed to continue practising Scottish Law independently of the English – and so it has remained to this day. Likewise, the Church of Scotland, which has its headquarters in Edinburgh, demanded as a prerequisite to the final signing of the Treaty of the Union of the Parliaments that it should retain full rights of independence.

On October 9th 2004, Queen Elizabeth II opened the New Scottish Parliament. The New Parliament does not occupy a single building but a series of buildings linked through the central Members' lobby with its pillars and sweeping roof lights. The Parliamentary Chamber, with its notable roof structure, is central to the whole complex. What is singular about the roof is the structure of oak beams that ascend and descend high above the Chamber, diminishing the height. Also, the outside landscape is plainly visible from within, symbolising the whole of Scotland. The architect, Enric

Miralles, internationally renowned for his work as one of the world's premier architects, had a vision for the Scottish Parliament as a building that sat in and grew out of the land, a building sympathetic to its historical setting but suitable for the 21st century. Nearby is the ancient building of the Palace of Holyroodhouse, within Holyrood Park. Behind the new Scottish Parliament are the comparatively new modern buildings of the Scotsman Publications and the Dynamic Earth exhibition. Sadly, the architect did not live to see the completion of the new Parliament Building. But the building has generated tremendous interest far and wide with its impressive ultra-modern architectural design.

Besides Holyrood Park, there are several other recreational areas in Edinburgh. One of particular interest is The Meadows, which lies to the south of the Old Town. Originally a loch surrounded by grassland where cattle and goats grazed, this stretch of land was reclaimed in 1722–40, and it thereafter became morally binding not to develop it. Another much-loved area is the Water of Leith, rising in the Pentlands Hills and running for about 20 miles through villages, with a gradual decline from some 1,250 ft as it winds its way through Edinburgh before flowing into the Firth of Forth at Leith. The Port of Leith used to be much busier when Leith was a separate town from Edinburgh, but it still handles significant freight and cruise vessels and is enjoying its renaissance as a centre for commerce and fine dining.

Another striking tale that emerged in Edinburgh is the story of the little Scots terrier Greyfriars Bobby. It came about, as so many true stories do, in a very unusual way. It happened that a policeman who lived in the Grassmarket wanted a sharp-nosed dog to help him track down criminals. A farmer provided him with such a dog , and it became the policeman's faithful little companion. They were devoted to one another as they worked together to find criminals. When the policeman died, the poor little dog was heartbroken, and refused to leave his master's grave in Greyfriars cemetery except for his dinner, which a local woman in the High Street continued to give him until he became too old. After that, a local publican would place a bowl of food outside his pub whenever the One O'clock

Gun went off, as it does every day at Edinburgh Castle. After his meal, the wee doggie would go back to his master's grave, growling protectively at anyone who dared come near. Eventually after 14 years (from1858 to 1872) he died on his master's grave. He now has his own gravestone placed next to his master. It is still believed by some that policemen thereafter were known as 'Bobbies' in respect of this faithful little doggie.

In spite of the many developments in and around Edinburgh, nothing can diminish the city's reputation for learning, or the magic of Arthur's Seat, or the quiet dignity of the Castle. Many visitors who capture its festive spirit go away with the feeling that Edinburgh is indeed a city to remember.

Elizabeth Fraser
February 2006

The Royal Mile & The Old Town

The elegance of this prestigious group of tenement houses belies their proximity to the bustle of the Royal Mile.

The flats of Ramsay Gardens are now amongst the most sought-after in the city.

Locals and visitors sauntering expectantly up the Royal Mile to the catch the first night of the Military Tattoo.

The Earl Haig Memorial and Ramsay Gardens, Castle Esplanade.

Ramsay Gardens were designed by Sir Patrick Geddes and built in 1892–3. They display a fusion of Scottish baronial and English cottage style, using red sandstone and whitewash in a dramatic location.

Back view of the top of the Royal Mile from Heriot's School.

A murky and chilling fog pervades the ghostly splendour of the impressive St Giles Cathedral. Consecrated by the Bishop of St Andrews in 1243, St Giles was funded mainly by Merchant Guilds, ship dues and fines.

The Mercat Cross was instigated and paid for by Prime Minister William Gladstone in 1885, and was originally the sight for proclamations and even executions.

Street theatre is a highly compelling aspect of the Festival. This Victorian doll moves with clockwork poise by Gladstone's Land.

The Fringe icon catches low sunshine outside the Festival shop on the Royal Mile.

The imposing statue of Alexander and Bucephalus rises in the fog to defend the City Chambers, The High Street.

The 'Mind Body Spirit' Shop in Cockburn Street steals the show on a misty night in the Old Town.

The West Bow (or Victoria Street)
has real style.

Victoria Street. Cafés on the balcony show an almost European flair.

From the foot of Candlemaker Row, looking up towards The Mound.

Edinburgh Castle from the Grassmarket.

Deacon Brodie's Tavern recalls the story of how the Deacon gained notoriety as one of the greatest hypocrites ever. Apparently an upstanding churchgoer on Sundays, he was a total scoundrel the rest of the week and a profligate gambler and thief – inspiration in fact for Robert Louis Stevenson's 'Dr Jekyll and Mr Hyde'.

Sidelight enhances the superb masonry of the Old Town buildings. The spire of St Giles Cathedral rises behind.

John Knox House, Canongate. The High Street was paved in 1533, and citizens were ordered to hang out lanterns at night.

Canongate Church dates back to 1688.

Chessels Court is tucked away off
The Canongate.

The tasteful colour scheme at Chessels Court, Canongate.

Back of the Canongate, from Regent Road.

The Tolbooth – courthouse, prison and punishment centre for over 300 years – has a striking clock tower between its two turrets.

The imposing Palace of Holyroodhouse is the official Scottish home of the Royal Family, and has seen nine centuries of pomp, glory and bloodshed.

Old Holyrood Abbey and the Palace in autumn sunlight.

Whitehorse Close at Abbey Strand, used as a Royal Mews in the 16th century, after which a merchant built an Inn and coaching stables here. Also used as the headquarters in the 1745 rebellion, it was restored in 1965.

Classical Times

Pillars of the National Gallery of Scotland.

The Scott Monument from Princes Street Gardens.

Edinburgh Castle from below in autumn.

The Cannon on Calton Hill.

A dusting of snow on the spire of the Balmoral Hotel enhances the intricate crafted detail on this most prominent of landmarks.

St Bernard's Well on the Water of Leith Walkway.

Classic New Town facade, Moray Place.

Statue of the Duke of Wellington and the Scott Monument at Register House.

Sculpture of Sir Walter Scott sheltering beneath his own monument. This phenomenal construction is probably the finest ever built to commemorate any writer in the world.

The Palm House, Royal Botanic Garden: Scotland's premier garden. Originally founded as a physic garden, it settled and expanded in Inverleith in 1820.

Upper Dean Terrace, New Town of Edinburgh.

The Ross Fountain and Edinburgh Castle from Princes Street Gardens.

The National Gallery of Scotland and the Mound.

Spires of the city at sunset through the memorial to Dugald Stewart from Calton Hill.

The National Monument on Calton Hill. A monument to the Scots who died in the Napoleonic Wars, it was started in 1822 but abandoned in 1830. These twelve magnificent Doric columns were all that was achieved.

New Town doorway, Henderson Row.

The steps leading past the National Gallery of Scotland to the Mound.

Donaldson's School, West Coates Terrace.

Fettes College.

George Heriot's School, Lauriston Place.

Edinburgh

The grand gates of the Palace of Holyroodhouse, wrought in iron and bronze. The gates were erected in 1922.

The bronze casting on George IV Bridge is a tribute to this world famous terrier who followed the remains of his master to Greyfriars churchyard and lingered on the spot until his death in 1872.

Greyfriars Church dates back to 1620 – and this view from the historic graveyard to the Old Town has perhaps changed little in that time.

The Scott Monument emanates great presence throughout Princes Street and beyond.

Grand Vistas

Edinburgh Castle rises majestically from the heart of the city. This is the view from the top of the Salisbury Crags.

The Commonwealth Pool and the Pollock Halls of Residence, from Arthur's Seat.

Nestling below Arthur's Seat is the wonderfully eclectic mix of buildings at Holyrood.

The Bridges, Salisbury Crags and Arthur's Seat under a dusting of snow.

Princes Street Gardens, Ramsay Gardens and the Castle from the Scott Monument.

On a wintry morning from the City Observatory, the city unfolds up to the great wall that is the Salisbury Crags.

Moonrise over Arthur's Seat and the Commonwealth Pool.

Probably the most familiar view of the city: from Calton Hill looking west.

North Bridge, the Balmoral Hotel and the Scott Monument.

A view from the summit of The Salisbury Crags, showing the dense mix of architecture that comprises the city.

From Calton Hill, looking to the Port of Leith.

The rear of the Castle as seen from the viewpoint on Blackford Hill very early one crisp winter's morning.

The Castle at dusk, from Arthur's Seat.

From whichever angle it is viewed, Princes Street is largely defined by spires. In late sun from Calton Hill.

The grand vista from The Scott Monument, looking west.

North Queensferry. A soft 'haar' (east coast morning mist) generates a romanticised impression of the great bridge.

The Forth Rail Bridge enjoys instant global recognition. The Road Bridge is also visible to the left.

From Bruntsfield Place, looking to the Castle.

The classical lines of the National Gallery of Scotland sit comfortably beneath the great dominance of the Castle.

Spring blossom and the Scott Monument from the Mound.

*Dusk behind the Balmoral Hotel
and Princes Street.*

The Scottish Parliament Building from the Radical Road.

Contemporary Times

Castle reflections in Saltire Court, Castle Terrace.

Drummers on parade at the Military Tattoo.

Post-rehearsal, these performers from the Tattoo burst happily onto the city streets.

Christmas shoppers heading home along Princes Street.

New residential development at Ronaldson's Wharf, Port of Leith.

Edinburgh

The Port of Leith has transformed into an exclusive enclave for trendy eateries.

Sandy Bell's pub on a foggy night.

The Scottish Parliament Building.

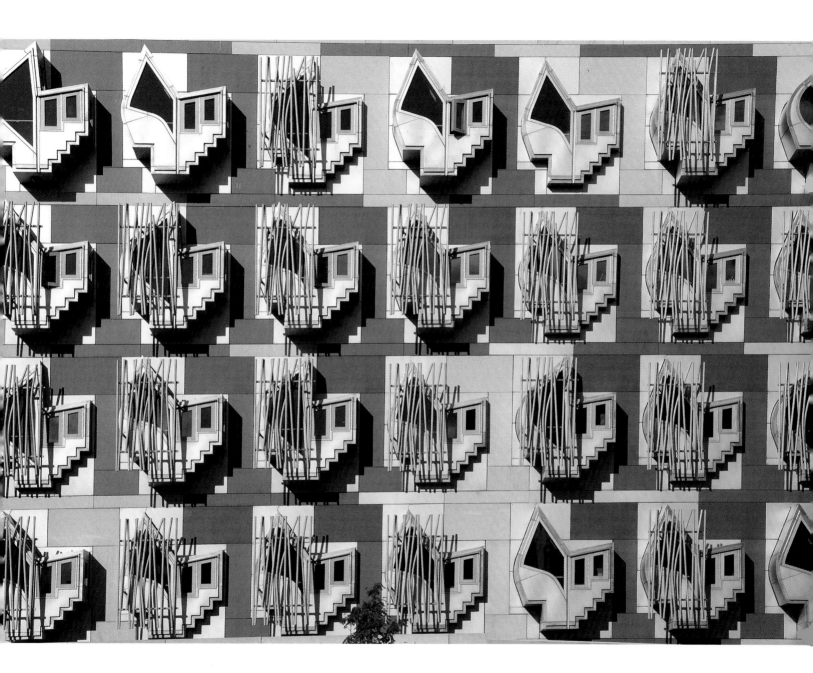

The casement windows of the Scottish Parliament.

The Edinburgh International Convention Centre.

Greyfriars Bobby and the National Museum of Scotland.

Finale of the Edinburgh Military Tattoo.

The Tattoo in full swing.

Classic tour bus passing the National Museum of Scotland.

Sightseeing bus and the Scott Monument at Waverley.

This mural was painted on a gable end in North Junction Street in 1986 by Tim Chalk and Paul Grime.

Lyrical lines invoke both the legacy and the smartness of the Shore, Port of Leith.

The Shore, Port of Leith.

Front of the Scottish Parliament Building from Horse Wynd.

Prestonfield House and golf course from Arthur's Seat.

Junior soccer on The Meadows one crisp Saturday morning.

Early dog-walking on Calton Hill.

The Forth Road Bridge.

The Burke and Hare Pub, West Port.

Singular Places

St Margaret's Loch, Holyrood Park, with St Anthony's Chapel on the hill.

The arched entrance to St Stephen's Place Market in Stockbridge.

Coronation Walk, The Meadows.

The Shore at the Port of Leith.

The Old Customs House, Albert Dock, Port of Leith.

The serene atmosphere of the Royal Botanic Gardens has been cherished by generations of citizens and visitors alike

The Rock Garden, early winter morning.

The less familiar but magnificent Craigmillar Castle stands bold in the winter sunshine.

Dean Village, once a successful milling community, now thrives again as a desirable residential zone.

Portobello promenade: a classic Victorian design.

The vernacular architecture of Newhaven, once a fishing community, has been lovingly restored.

The stylish rear of Barclay Church faces The Meadows and displays the best traditions of the Scottish Presbyterian style.

North Bridge and the Balmoral Hotel from Market Street. This illustrious viaduct, first built in 1772, embodies the great care the city takes of its finest architectural heritage.

Brilliant spring sunshine creates an explosion of colour among the Azaleas in the Royal Botanic Garden.

Visitors relax in the late summer sun on the mock Parthenon pillars of the National Monument on Calton Hill.

Sandy Bell's bar: a famous watering hole with live music, Forrest Road.

Red door and two pigeons, Robb Close, Cowgate.

Elaborate railings and towering chimneys: George IV Bridge from the Cowgate.

The city by night from the rooftops of Ramsay Gardens.

The Shore at the Port of Leith is now experiencing a major renaissance as a stylish dining and commercial enclave

Casement windows to the rear of the Scottish Parliament building.

Parliament Square, behind St Giles Cathedral.